CCSS Genre Exposito

Essential Ques
How do Earth's forces affect us?

MW00682223

FORCES AT WORK

by Beverly Harris

PAIRED READ Machines to Push and Pull .. 17

A **force** pushes or pulls things.

Push a swing. Pull a wagon.
The force makes them move.

Gravity is a force. It pulls things to Earth. Throw a ball. It falls down not up!

pushing force

friction

Friction is a force. **Rub** two things together. You made friction! Friction slows things down.

You can see forces at work.
This girl sits on a slide.
Gravity pulls her down.
Friction slows her **speed**.

Kick a ball. It rubs the grass. Friction slows the ball.

This shoe digs into the ground. It makes friction. Now, it won't slip.

McGraw-Hill Companies Inc./Ken Cavanagh, Photographer

Even the air makes friction.
It slows the ball.

Friction helps a skater push off.

The stopper **drags** on the ground. That makes friction. The skates slow down.

How can the bike stop?
Use the **brakes**. They **grab**
the wheels. That makes
friction. The bike will stop.

Why does a football go so fast? Its shape makes **less** friction with the air.

Swimmers use caps and suits. These are **smooth**. Smooth things make less friction with the water. That way swimmers can go fast!

Forces are everywhere!

Respond to Reading

Summarize

Summarize *Forces at Work.* The chart may help you.

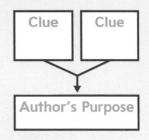

Text Evidence

1. Why do you think the author wrote this book? Author's Purpose

2. Read the word *suits* on page 14. Use the words and pictures. How can you tell what *suits* are?

   Vocabulary

3. Write about the forces in a soccer game. Write About Reading

Compare Texts

Machines help us push and pull.

Machines to Push and Pull

Gravity gives objects weight.
We can measure weight.
Some things are heavy.
They are hard to move.

Machines are tools. They
help us work against gravity.
Amazing!

Force	Push	Pull
Moving a grocery cart	X	
Playing Tug-of-War game		X
Hitting a baseball	X	

The workers use a ramp to move the piano safely.

A ramp is a simple machine. One end is on the ground. The other is lifted up. People can slide a heavy object up the ramp. That is easier than lifting it.

A lever is a simple machine, too. It helps lift heavy things. A wheelbarrow is a lever.

The man uses the handles to move the wheelbarrow.

Make Connections

What does gravity do?

Essential Question

Is there friction when you use a wheelbarrow? Text to Text

Focus on
Science

Purpose To see friction at work

What to Do

Step 1 ▶ Work with a partner. Get a toy car with wheels and a wooden block.

Step 2 ▶ Push the car on the floor. Now push the block. Use the same force. Does the car or the block go farther?

Conclusion Tell how pushing the two things shows friction at work.